We Walk to School

Staying Strong and Healthy

We walk to school.

3

We walk past the park.

We walk past the shops.

We walk past the clock.

9

We walk past the church.

SUNDAY WORSHIP **9.30 am**
HOLY COMMUNION 1ST SUNDAY

THIS AUTUMN, THANK GOD
FOR "ALL THINGS BRIGHT
& BEAUTIFUL" !

11

We walk past the **statue.**

We walk past the **bridge.**

bridge

statue